9 8 7 6
Digit on the right indicates the number of this printing

Library of Congress Control Number: 2013954434

ISBN 978-0-7624-5386-3

Running Press Book Publishers
A Member of the Perseus Books Group
2300 Chestnut Street
Philadelphia, PA 19103-4371

Visit us on the web!
www.runningpress.com

CONTENTS

INTRODUCTION

WILLIAM SHAKESPEARE IS THE
most studied writer in the history
of Western civilization. His body of
work includes thirty-eight plays,
154 sonnets, and two epic narrative
poems. And it's not like he lived to
be 100, or anything. But even if he
had, I think we can all agree that
the man was insanely prolific—and
wildly successful in his lifetime.

To the people of Elizabethan England, he was a rock star. Think of the popularity of J. K. Rowling, Oprah Winfrey, Elvis, and the Beatles—*combined*.

Even if you've never read any of Shakespeare's works, you've probably quoted him countless times without even knowing it. His words are so timeless, so universal that, over the centuries, they have seamlessly integrated into our lexicon.

Surely you've called something "a sorry sight." That's from *Macbeth,* as is "as pure as the driven snow." Bet the last time you said that you hadn't "slept one wink," you didn't realize you were quoting *Cymbeline.* Ever been "in a pickle"? Well, so was Trinculo in *The Tempest.* And a "wild goose chase"? That one's from *Romeo and Juliet.*

But most importantly—for our purposes, anyway—Shakespeare

was king of the comeback. His more temper-prone characters— from Hamlet to Shylock to Lady Macbeth to just about any and all of the King Henrys—didn't hold their tongues when they were annoyed, hardly ever hesitating before doling out verbal lashings left and right. And yes, he will go *there* . . . openly issuing jabs at beauty (or lack thereof), bodily odors, and practically initiating the "your momma . . ." insult that still prevails on elementary school playgrounds to this day.

For all of Shakespeare's words and phrases that are still in frequent use today, there are still many more that have, sadly, fallen by the wayside over the past 400 years. Let's bring them back: knave, churl, white liver'd, sodden-witted, beef-witted, and, of course, a bull's pizzle. Try tossing out one of these next time you find yourself in a heated discussion, and then, well, it'll pretty much be checkmate for you, my friend.

Evidently, Shakespeare garnered envy early on for his talent and success—critic Robert Greene referred to him in 1892 as "an upstart Crow"—but his biting wit and dexterity with insults surely left more than one of these critics speechless. From attacks on boorishness to stinging critiques of character and false faith, the masterfully composed affronts are deftly integrated into his plays, securing Shakespeare's spot as the sixteenth century's master of repartee--and bringing welcome moments of levity to even the darkest and most tragic of his tragedies.

Presented here are 133 razor-sharp gibes straight from the pen of the Bard himself. The insults and jabs that peppered his plays are neatly compiled—and strategically organized by topic, for super-quick reference—in this handy, portable tome. Whether you're dealing with an imbecile, a hypocrite, an egoist, an unwelcome flirt, a villain, any sort of pest—or any combination of these—with this book, you'll never find yourself without a comeback again.

THE LIFE OF
WILLIAM
SHAKESPEARE

IN 1623, DRAMATIST BEN JONSON said of Shakespeare: "He was not of an age, but for all time." Boy was that a keen and prescient observation, but perhaps even Jonson would be surprised by just how widely read Shakespeare's plays are more than 400 years after they were written—or by the lingering potency of his still-scathing insults.

We actually don't know too much about William Shakespeare's life (definitively speaking), aside from information found in public records. The son of John Shakespeare (a successful glove maker and community leader who later fell upon hard times) and Mary (Arden) Shakespeare (daughter of a wealthy landowner), William was baptized in Stratford, England (about ninety miles outside of London), on April 26, 1564. He was their third child, but the first to make it out of infancy alive. Although no school records from this time exist, most agree that due to his relatively well-to-do family, it is likely that Shakespeare was a student at King Edward VI Grammar School in Stratford, where he would have learned Latin and literature. There are no records indicating his having attended university.

In 1582, Shakespeare married Anne Hathaway, a farmer's daughter who was 26 and already pregnant with their first child at the time of their union. He was only eighteen at the time, which was considered a minor, so the marriage required the written consent of his parents. Daughter Susanna was born on May 26, 1583. Twins

Hamnet and Judith followed less than two years later on February 2, 1585. (Sadly, Hamnet later died at age 11.) They had no more children, most likely due to the fact that Shakespeare soon after moved to London—then a thriving city of between 150,000 and 200,000 residents and where he would live over the next twenty years—leaving his family behind in Stratford, though still taking care of them financially. He even took care of his folks, likely paying the fees for his father to be granted a family coat of arms in 1596.

What exactly Shakespeare was doing (and where) between the years 1585 and 1592 is somewhat of a mystery, leading many scholars to refer to this period as "the lost years." Speculation regarding what he may have spent those years doing includes: traveling the continent; studying law; teaching; and apprenticing with a butcher.

We do know, though, that by the time 1592 rolled around, he had written at least three plays, one of which—*Henry VI, Part I*—was a smashing success, performed nightly to audiences of between 2,000 and 3,000 people. Half of these attendees stood (for many hours!) and were called "groundlings." The rest of the audience sat in more expensive seats in three galleries.

Shakespeare first garnered wide

recognition for his poetry, though, and his very first publication was a nearly 1,200-line poem called *Venus and Adonis* in 1593, which was wildly popular. It was dedicated to his patron, Henry Wriothesley, the Earl of Southampton. The earl was young, wealthy, literary minded, and apparently bisexual. Naturally, there is much speculation as to the true nature of his relationship with Shakespeare. Were they lovers?

In the early and mid 1590s, Shakespeare was a rising star—as an actor and playwright—in London's bustling theater scene. Unfortunately, in that same year, the theaters in London were ordered to be closed down and remained closed for nearly two years, due to a nasty outbreak of the plague.

During this downtime, Shakespeare played a key role in the organization of a theater company called Lord Chamberlain's Men, which was renamed the King's Men in 1603 (in honor of King James I's ascent to the throne after Queen Elizabeth I's death). The center of this scene was a playhouse called the Theatre, which was succeeded by the Globe, which later opened in 1599.

Despite his "rising star" status, Shakespeare wasn't officially (in print) credited with authorship of his plays (since it was customary for them to be attributed to theater companies, not individuals) until 1597, with *Richard III*. He spent the 1590s writing mostly his histories and comedies, concentrating on his tragedies later, in the 1600s.

In 1609, Shakespeare published a volume of his 154 sonnets (believed to have been written at the same time as his earlier poetry, more than ten years before). Proving the timelessness of literary critics having too much time on their hands, these sonnets have been scrutinized over the years for insight into the somewhat mysterious life of Shakespeare. The first 126 of the sonnets were written to the "beautiful boy," whom many believe to be William Herbert, the young Earl of Pembroke and son of one of Shakespeare's patrons. Were they lovers? There is no conclusive proof either way.

The last twenty-eight of the sonnets were written for a "Dark Lady," thought to have been Emilia Lanier, a beautiful young woman with whom Shakespeare is thought to have had an affair. (Incidentally, Emilia later went on to be the first woman to publish a volume of her own poetry in England.) Some even speculate that perhaps Shakespeare, Herbert, and Emilia were all involved in some sort of sordid love triangle.

Again, though, there is no conclusive proof of this.

One thing's for sure: Shakespeare brought an art form (poetry and drama) originally intended for the elite, for royalty, to a much wider audience. Along the way, he coined more than 2,000 new words or phrases, including the witty-but-brutal insults featured in this book.

It's believed that after more than twenty years in London,

Shakespeare returned to Stratford around 1610, where he lived until his death in April of 1616—some say on his fifty-second birthday. He is buried in the Holy Trinity Church in Stratford. (Anne lived another seven years and was buried beside the husband she barely ever saw.)

The first collection of his works—known as the First Folio—appeared seven years later, in 1623. (In 2009, an original edition of the First Folio sold for nearly five million dollars at auction!)

With his personal life somewhat mysterious, some have theorized that perhaps Shakespeare's plays were actually written by a group of men or someone else entirely. Particularly suspect was the fact that Shakespeare never attended university. How could have an uneducated man have written so prolifically, so beautifully? Of course, such an assumption is ridiculous. Nonetheless, some of the names bandied about over the centuries as possible collaborators or ghost writers are fellow poet and dramatist Christopher Marlowe; statesman and philosopher (a Renaissance Man, really) Sir Francis Bacon; and even the Virgin Queen, herself, Elizabeth I. Though these notions can be neither definitely confirmed nor denied, they are dismissed by most as mere conspiracy theories.

But enough about the play-wright, himself. Let's get on to the good stuff!

BEAUTY
and
BOORISHNESS

Thou crusty batch of nature.

—Troilus and Cressida

Bolting-hutch
of beastliness.

—*Henry IV, Part I*

Thou lump of foul deformity!

—Richard III

I HAVE SEEN BETTER
FACES IN MY TIME
THAN STANDS ALONE
ON ANY SHOULDER
THAT I SEE BEFORE ME
AT THIS INSTANT.

—*King Lear*

The tartness of his face sours ripe grapes.

—*Coriolanus*

This sanguine coward,
this bed-presser,
this horseback-breaker,
this huge hill of flesh!

—*Henry IV, Part I*

Thou

ELVISH-MARK'D, ABORTIVE, ROOTING HOG.

—*Richard III*

His intellect
is not replenished,
he is only an animal,
only sensible in the
duller parts.

—*Love's Labour's Lost*

Thou
smell of
mountain
goat.

—*Henry V*

SHE IS SPHERICAL,

LIKE A GLOBE.

I COULD FIND OUT

COUNTRIES IN HER.

—*The Comedy of Errors*

You peasant swain!
You whoreson
malt-horse drudge!

—The Taming of the Shrew

When he is best,
he is a little worse than a man,
and when he is worst

he is little better
than a beast.

—*The Merchant of Venice*

THY MOTHER
TOOK INTO HER
BLAMEFUL BED
SOME STERN
UNTUTOR'D CHURL . . .
WHOSE FRUIT
THOU ART . . .

—*Henry VI, Part II*

Scratching could
not make it worse...
such a face as yours.

—*Much Ado About Nothing*

Could I come
near your beauty
with my nails
I'd set my ten
commandments
in your face.

—*Henry VI, Part II*

Thou

CREAM-FACED LOON.
WHERE GOT'ST
THAT GOOSE LOOK?

—*Macbeth*

There is not ugly a fiend of hell as thou shalt be ...

—*King John*

He is
white-liver'd
and
red-fac'd.

—*Henry V*

OUT,
YOU GREEN-SICKNESS
CARRION!
OUT,
YOU BAGGAGE!
YOU TALLOW FACE!

—*Romeo and Juliet*

How ill white hairs
become a fool
and a jester!...
So surfeit-swell'd,
so old and so profane.

—*Henry VI, Part II*

He is
deformed, crooked,
old, and sere,
Ill-faced, worse bodied,
shapeless everywhere;
Vicious, ungentle, foolish,
blunt, unkind;
Stigmatical in making,
worse in mind.

—*The Comedy of Errors*

YOUR BREATH FIRST
KINDLED THE
DEAD COALS OF WARS . . .
AND BROUGHT IN MATTER
THAT SHOULD FEED THIS FIRE;
AND NOW 'TIS FAR TOO HUGE
TO BE BLOWN OUT
WITH THAT SAME WEAK WIND
WHICH ENKINDLED IT.

—*King John*

Most smiling,
smooth, detested
parasites, courteous
destroyers, affable
wolves, meek bears...

—Timon of Athens

Out of my sight!
Thou dost
infect my eyes.

—*Richard III*

MARK

the FLEERS,

GIBES *and*

NOTABLE SCORNS

THAT DWELL *in*

EVERY REGION

of HIS FACE.

—*Othello*

INTELLECT
and
SPEECH

Hide not thy poison with such sugar'd words.

—*Henry VI, Part II*

If thou speak'st false,
upon the next tree
shalt thou hang alive,
till famine cling thee.

—*Macbeth*

IF I PROVE HONEY-MOUTH'D, LET MY TONGUE BLISTER.

—The Winter's Tale

More of your conversation would infect my brain.

—*Coriolanus*

"I know
what I know."

"I can hardly
believe that, since
you know not what
you speak."

—*Measure for Measure*

A FUSTY NUT

with

NO KERNEL.

—*Troilus and Cressida*

A fellow of no mark nor likelihood.

—Henry IV, Part I

My tongue
will tell
the anger
of my heart.

—*The Taming of the Shrew*

BETTER A WITTY FOOL
THAN A FOOLISH WIT.

—Twelfth-Night

Your wit makes wise things foolish.

—Love's Labour's Lost

Take you me for a sponge?

—*Hamlet*

THE MOTIONS OF
HIS SPIRIT ARE
AS DULL AS NIGHT.

—The Merchant of Venice

I was
searching
for a
fool when
I found you.

—*As You Like It*

He's winding up
the watch
of his wit;
by and by
it will strike.

—*The Tempest*

HAVE YOUR MOUTH FILL'D UP BEFORE YOU OPEN IT.

—*Henry VIII*

You abilities
are too
infant-like
for doing
much alone.

—*Coriolanus*

You
are not worth
another word.

—*Twelfth-Night*

THOU SODDEN-WITTED
LORD! THOU HAST NO
MORE BRAIN THAN I
HAVE IN MINE ELBOWS.

—*Troilus and Cressida*

You
talk greasily,
your lips
grow foul.

—Love's Labour's Lost

He has not
so much
brain
as ear-wax.

—*Troilus and Cressida*

THERE'S A MAN HATH
MORE HAIR THAN WIT.

—*The Comedy of Errors*

It is a tale
told by an idiot,
full of sound
and fury,
signifying
nothing.

—*Macbeth*

Thou
whoreson,
senseless villain!

—*The Comedy of Errors*

YOUR WIT
WILL NOT SO SOON
OUT AS ANOTHER
MAN'S WILL;
'TIS STRONG WEDGED
UP IN A BLOCKHEAD.

—*Coriolanus*

Thou hast no more brain than I have in my elbows.

—Troilus and Cressida

A false *and* dull-eyed fool.

—*The Merchant of Venice*

THE PLAGUE
OF GREECE UPON THEE,
THOU MONGREL
BEEF-WITTED LORD!

—Troilus and Cressida

RELIGION
and
BLASPHEMY

There is no more faith in thee than in a stewed prune.

—*Henry IV, Part I*

Heaven
truly knows that
thou art
false as hell.

—*Othello*

THERE IS NO MORE
MERCY IN HIM
THAN THERE IS MILK
IN A MALE TIGER.

—*Coriolanus*

He wears his
faith but as the
fashion of his hat;
it ever changes
with the next
block.

—*Much Ado About Nothing*

A fiend like thee
might bear
my soul to hell.

—*Twelfth-Night*

O FAITHLESS COWARD!

O DISHONEST WRETCH!

WILT THOU BE MADE

A MAN OUT OF MY VICE?

—*Measure for Measure*

Get thee to a nunnery!

—Hamlet

Thou art
unfit for
any place
but hell.

—*Richard III*

AN EVIL SOUL
PRODUCING HOLY
WITNESS IS LIKE
A VILLAIN WITH
A SMILING CHEEK,
A GOODLY APPLE ROTTEN
AT THE HEART.

—*The Merchant of Venice*

Ye have
angels' faces,
but heaven
knows your
hearts.

—*Henry VIII*

The devil
hath power to assume
a pleasing shape.

—*Hamlet*

SUPPOSED SINCERE

AND HOLY IN HIS

THOUGHTS . . .

DERIVES FROM HEAVEN

HIS QUARREL

AND HIS CAUSE.

—*Henry IV, Part II*

Thou monstrous injurer of heaven and earth!

—*King John*

Idol
of
idiot-
worshippers.

—*Troilus and Cressida*

EARTH GAPES,

HELL BURNS,

FIENDS ROAR,

SAINTS PRAY,

TO HAVE HIM

SUDDENLY

COVEY'D AWAY.

—*Richard III*

go to hell
for an eternal
moment or so.

—The Merry Wives of Windsor

There's two
of you; the devil
make a third!

—*Henry VI, Part I*

HIS CURSES
AND BLESSINGS
TOUCH ME ALIKE;
THEY'RE BREATH
I NOT BELIEVE IN.

—*Henry VIII*

Chide God for making you the countenance you are.

—As You Like It

LOVE
and
LUST

Many a good hanging prevents a bad marriage.

—Twelfth-Night

She
adulterates
hourly.

—*King John*

DISSEMBLING HARLOT, THOU ART FALSE IN ALL!

—The Comedy of Errors

...She's a bed-swerver.

—The Winter's Tale

'Tis the
strumpet's
plague
to beguile many
and be beguiled
by one.

—*Othello*

HE IS GIVEN

TO SPORTS,

TO WILDNESS

and

MUCH COMPANY.

—*Julius Caesar*

HAG

of

ALL

DESPITE!

—*Henry VI, Part I*

That kiss
is comfortless as
frozen water to a
starved snake.

—*Titus Andronicus*

I HAD RATHER HEAR MY DOG

BARK AT A CROW THAN

A MAN SWEAR HE LOVES ME.

—*Much Ado About Nothing*

O curse of marriage, that we can call these delicate creatures ours, and not their appetites.

—Othello

Thou
mis-shapen Dicke!

—Henry VI, Part III

I DO REPENT

THE TEDIOUS

MINUTES

I WITH

HER HAVE SPENT.

—*A Midsummer-Night's Dream*

She is ill-met by moonlight.

—A Midsummer-Night's Dream

If she should make
tender of her love,
'tis very possible
he'll scorn it;
for the man, as you
know all, hath a
contemptible spirit.

—*Much Ado About Nothing*

HE DID LOVE HER,
SIR, AS A GENTLEMAN
LOVES A WOMAN...
HE LOVE HER, SIR,
AND LOVER HER NOT.

—*All's Well that Ends Well*

Such is the simplicity of man to harken after the flesh.

—Love's Labour's Lost

...An adulterous
thief, a hypocrite,
a virgin-violator.

—*Measure for Measure*

She has

BEEN SLUICED

IN'S ABSENCE

AND HIS POND FISHE'D

by his

NEXT NEIGHBOUR.

—*The Winter's Tale*

Being no other but as she is, I do not like her.

—*Much Ado About Nothing*

CHARACTER and VILLAINY

Thou art a wickedness.

—Twelfth-Night

Thou art a most
notable coward,
an infinite
and endless liar,
an hourly promise
breaker, the owner of not
one good quality.

—*All's Well that Ends Well*

AWAY,
YOU CUT-PURSE
RASCAL,
YOU FILTHY BUNG,
AWAY!

—*Henry IV, Part II*

In civility thou seem'st so empty.

—As You Like It

There's neither honesty, manhood, not good fellowship in thee.

—*Henry IV, Part I*

Are you like
THE PAINTING OF

A SORROW,

A FACE

WITHOUT A HEART?

—*Hamlet*

Son and heir of a mongrel bitch.

—*King Lear*

Out, dunghill!

—King John

YOU JUGGLER!
you
CANKER-BLOSSOM!

—*A Midsummer Night's Dream*

Pernicious blood-sucker of sleeping men.

—*Henry VI, Part II*

Bloody,
bawdy villain!
Remorseless,
treacherous,
lecherous,
kindless villain.

—*Hamlet*

SUCH IS THY
AUDACIOUS
WICKEDNESS,
THY LEWD,
PESTIFEROUS AND
DISSENTIOUS PRANKS,
AS VERY INFANTS
PRATTLE OF THY PRIDE.

—Henry VI, Part I

The villainy you teach
me I will execute,
and it shall go hard
but I will better
the instruction.

—*The Merchant of Venice*

O
thou
vile one!

—*Cymbeline*

I DO HATE THEE

WORSE THAN

A PROMISE-BREAKER.

—*Coriolanus*

You are
not
worth
the dust
which the rude
wind blows in
your face.

—*King Lear*

Thou are so leaky
that we much leave
thee to thy sinking.

—*Antony and Cleopatra*

Thou
WHORESON ZED!
Thou
UNNECESSARY

LETTER!

—*King Lear*

Words are easy,
like the wind,
Faithful friends
are hard to find.

—*Passionate Pilgrim*

Away!
Thou'rt poison
to my blood.

—Cymbeline

I think he be

TRANSFORMED INTO A
BEAST, FOR I CAN NO WHERE
FIND HIM LIKE A MAN.

—*As You Like It*

You are strangely troublesome.

—*Henry VIII*

I do desire
we may be
**better
strangers.**

—*As You Like It*

A FORTUNE-TELLER,

A NEEDY,

HOLLOW-EYED,

SHARP-LOOKING

WRETCH,

A LIVING DEAD MAN.

—*The Comedy of Errors*

His humor is lofty, his discourse peremptory, his tongue filed, his eye ambitious, his gait majestical and his general behavior vain, ridiculous, and thrasonical. He is too picked, too spruce, too affected, too odd, as it were, too peregrinate, as I may call it.

—Love's Labour's Lost

Bastard begot,
bastard
instructed,
bastard in mind,...
in everything
illegitimate.

—*Troilus and Cressida*

'SBLOOD,
YOU STARVELING,
YOU ELF-SKIN, YOU DRIED
NEAT'S TONGUE,
YOU BULL'S PIZZLE,
YOU STOCK-FISH!
O FOR BREATH TO UTTER
WHAT IS LIKE THEE!
YOU TAILOR'S-YARD,
YOU SHEATH, YOU BOWCASE;
YOU VILE STANDING-TUCK!

—*Henry IV, Part I*

Go hang yourself, you naughty mocking uncle!

—Troilus and Cressida

His treasons will sit
blushing in his face.

—Richard II

One

MAY SMILE,

AND SMILE,

AND BE

A VILLAIN.

—*Hamlet*

Avaunt, you cullions!

—Henry V

We make guilty of our
disasters the sun, the moon,
and the stars, as if we were
villains by necessity, fools by
heavenly compulsion.

—*King Lear*

One

WHOSE HARD HEART

IS BUTTONED UP

WITH STEEL ...

PITILESS AND ROUGH ...

—*The Comedy of Errors*

Away, you mouldy rogue, away!

—Henry IV, Part II

Thou are sick in the
world's regard, wretched
and low, a poor unminded
outlaw sneaking home.

—*Henry V*

FROM THE
EXTREMEST UPWARD
OF THY HEAD TO THE
DESCENT AND DUST
BENEATH THY FOOT,
A MOST TOAD
SPOTTER TRAITOR.

—*King Lear*

I had rather
chop this hand off
at a blow,
And with the other
fling it at thy face.

—*Henry VI, Part III*

Take away
this villain;
shut him up.

—*Love's Labour's Lost*

Thou bitch-wolf's son!

—Troilus and Cressida

This book has been bound
using handcraft methods and Smyth-
sewn to ensure durability.

Designed by Amanda Richmond.

The text was compiled and
edited by Nancy Armstrong,
Catherine Sweeney, and Joelle Herr.

The text was set in Chronicle,
Black Knight, and Dear Alison.